UNFINISHED CITY

Unfinished City

Poems

Nan Cohen

Nan Cohen

For David with love from Nan

Gunpowder Press • Santa Barbara
2017

Published by Gunpowder Press
David Starkey, Editor
PO Box 60035
Santa Barbara, CA 93160-0035

Cover image: Pieter Bruegel the Elder, *Tower of Babel*
            (KHM-Museumsverband, Vienna)
Back cover photo: Annahstasia Enuke
ISBN-13: 978-0-9986458-0-3

www.gunpowderpress.com

For Matthew

ACKNOWLEDGEMENTS

Grateful acknowledgment is made to the editors of the following publications, where these poems appeared, sometimes in slightly different form:

The Forward: "Eve in the Garden" (as "Pruning")

Grasslands Review: "Ordeals by Water" and "Ambulance"

Gulf Coast: "It Is Not in the Heavens, Neither is it Beyond the Sea"

The New Republic: "Storm"

Jews.: "In the Unfinished City"

Pilgrimage: "Bee 2"

Ploughshares: "Abraham and Isaac: I" and "Abraham and Isaac: II"

Slate: "The Fear of the Dark"

Southern California Review: "Mother Eve" (as "Eve")

Wind: "Plague of Darkness"

"Egg" appeared in *Lounge Lit* (LitRhap Press, 2005), edited by Tess. Lotta, Wendy C. Ortiz, and Andrea Quaid, and received a 2005 Dorothy Sargent Rosenberg Award.

Contents

1. Eve's Childhood

Eve's Childhood	13
Egg	14
Bee 1	15
Depth Perception	16
Unfinished City	17
Jacob and the Angel	18
Tamar	19
Storm	20
Ordeals by Water	21
Birth	22

2. It Is Not in the Heavens, Neither Is It Beyond the Sea

Mother Eve	25
A Cry Over Water	26
Bee 2: Individual	27
Burning Bush	28
First Fruit	29
It is Not in the Heavens, Neither Is It Beyond the Sea	30
Abraham and Isaac: I	31
Abraham and Isaac: II	32
Plague of Darkness	33
Crossing	34
Talion	35
Alive into Sheol	36
The Fear of the Dark	37

Chocolate   38

Manna   39

Turning Forty   40

Alien Fire   41

Envy   42

Ashes   43

Jethro   44

Journey/Sojourn   45

Emor   46

3. A PAIR OF SHEARS

Eve in the Garden   49

Spiderweb Elegy   50

A Pair of Shears   51

Bee 3   52

On the Past   53

On Being in Other People's Dreams   55

Ambulance   57

Inquiry   58

Concerning Your Death   59

Mount Nebo   60

Ha'azinu   61

The LORD came down to look at the city and tower which man had built, and the LORD said, "If, as one people with one language for all, this is how they have begun to act, then nothing they may propose to do will be out of their reach.

"Let us, then, go down and confound their speech there, so that they shall not understand one another's speech."

Thus the LORD scattered them from there over the face of the whole earth; and they stopped building the city.

That is why it was called Babel, because there the LORD confounded the speech of the whole earth; and from there the LORD scattered them over the face of the whole earth.

Genesis 11:5-9

1.

EVE'S CHILDHOOD

With what shall I approach the Eternal?

Micah 6.6

Eve's Childhood

Of course I had one, just like you:
like you, I know that someone said my name to me,
many times, every day, until it hooked
onto something inside and was my name;
like you, I didn't know I was a child,
and then I knew I was one;
like you, turned my face to the light
then turned away, and what I came
to know as colors and shapes

resolved themselves into things, those things acquired names,
my hands went out and felt them—

then curved around an apple, round and blazing like the sun,
red, dappled with yellow, every cell packed with fragrance,
every cell packed with sweetness, too late to stop that hurtling
toward the world, I had to keep going, to taste the names, to bite,
to speak my one sweet sentence: you felt it too, you know you did.

Egg

A child stands at the table to watch
the raw egg fall from its just-cracked shell.
She will beg to crack the egg herself,
then strike the bowl too lightly or too hard.
She has not yet seen hundreds of golden yolks
robed in glossy albumen, or endless
weekly cartons of eggs like brittle heads;
is not yet someone who doesn't thrill
to the shell rending, or who expertly
strikes the bowl with it, parts the crack
with delicate fingers. Only this child, this moment,
reaches for this breaking egg, this morning.

Bee 1

A honeybee, dusted with pollen,
pushing her head deeply
into a white flower.

Is me, pushing my head into this moment
as if I could live in it forever.

As if I could become, not just this—
but the idea of—a white flower.

As if I were, not just this—
but the idea of—honeybee.

As if I were not standing here, watching
bee enter flower, flower enfold bee.

Depth Perception

Eyes look out like pairs of lovers,
wanting to see the same landscape, but
forced, regardless, to occupy
      different angles.

One eye's view can only
match the other's imperfectly:
failing barely to meet, an accidental
      double exposure.

So when you open your eyes, the optic
nerve flares, the river heaves and turns over,
and what your right eye sees—a snowy egret
      flying above a

moving river—and what your left eye
sees—a snowy egret flying above
a moving river—meet in you, becoming
      fused in your cortex:

Egret flying, river. Something
neither left nor right has seen alone. They
made it together. It can't be unmade, and
      can't be forgotten.

Unfinished City

Passing the house where you once lived, I found
no change I could discern, and so I mourned.
Had something changed, I'd have mourned that too.

But why should bricks and mortar, plumbing, plaster,
laths, electrical wiring have such permanence
when you've left no memento of your presence,
which in its time was solid and complete?

Complete and solid in me lies your absence
since that wretched day when language broke apart
and what I spoke was sensible to me
and what you spoke was sensible to you

but neither understood the other's speech.
Lovingly I took your words into my mouth,
but they were foreign. I had to spit them out.

Jacob and the Angel

I will not let you go unless you bless me
Genesis 32:36

There was a love that tore the heart;
there were questions, too many to answer.

The sun comes next,
the long night's struggle ends.

You walked into the ocean,
asked it not to drown you;

you hoped the moon would keep you warm,
and yet you're here, alive,

not less foolish, but wiser.

Tamar

There's a heaviness in me
like a quickened child.
I am fertile with my burden,

I am barren with it.
I feed it my life,
but it takes my clothes, my voice,
every accustomed gesture,

keeps drawing my thoughts
to the one who is lost—
I fear there is no proof
he ever existed,

despite these clothes, the scraps
of paper from his pockets.
The sagging shoulders of a coat,
a pocket calendar—
All empty! And I,
married to a ghost, half ghost myself:

Oh, I eat—
then wash the plate
a thousand meals have vanished from.

Storm

It should be shelved in the absolute
library of amazement:

an encyclopedia in twelve volumes,
with a whole page
on the darkness of the soaked earth
in its bare patch by the door,
a section to the hanging leaf
with its coating of moisture,
one drop gathering down at the tip.

Another to the broken arms of branches,
the way the raw wood inside,
exposed, is already
starting to weather.

One volume to sounds of the air,
for where are they now, the sheets of wind,
blasts of thunder, awful silence of lightning?

Another to sounds of the earth,
the many tappings and batterings of rain,
the unlatched gate slapping the fence.

An appendix addressing the emotions themselves:
awareness of imminent grief, the grief itself.

Ordeals by Water

Before some great change, always as it was in the beginning,
with a darkness over the surface of the deep
and a wind from God sweeping over the water—

before some great change, the darkness is doubled,
night hovers over, mystery swims beneath.
Outside the body, particles of dusk soften the air;

the eyes see night coming on, the pupil dilates one millimeter
independent of thought or intention.

Inside the body, another body.
With a sudden lunge it has turned and thrust out its feet.
The amnion bulges gently, a bag of waters.

They came there drop by drop.
The body directed some of its waters there
and one day they rose and lifted like a tide.

Without intent, without volition.
A great change going on so slowly,
in the darkness within, in the darkness without.

Can a person change
so the good water will turn
bitter in her mouth?

Can she drink the bitter water,
make it sweet?

Birth

It was August the day was hot
too hot for tears but the tears came out
the water was calm the water was wide

It was September the day was hot
the boat was heaving waves leaped the side
inside the motion another motion

It was October the day was hot
the body surged it surged like a tide
out of the ocean another ocean

2.

IT IS NOT IN THE HEAVENS, NEITHER IS IT BEYOND THE SEA

...the thing is very close to you, in your mouth and in your heart, to observe it

Deuteronomy 30:14

Mother Eve

1.

When my body forced the child out
I drew him into my arms and felt my warmth
cooling from him, and his own beginning;
and the child looked at me and I was pierced
by his look:

                       it was pure and not amazed,
it was naked, it was perfectly intent,

and I thought: We are still loved,
we must be loved still;

and I thought I knew what He knew when,
the world begun, He spoke and heard
a small, new answering sound.

2.

But I have never seen creation.
Only what is created.
Did not hear the first sound
of the answering voice.
I have never seen destruction;

only what is destroyed, forced
out of itself, into ash, into rubble;

Into the body lying lifeless,
sight fled from the eyes,
strength fled from the hand.

A Cry Over Water

Exodus 2:6

Comes at dawn from a rocking basket
and carries, looking for a resting place.

The cry curls over the waters of the night,
seeking a soft ear to crawl inside.

Admit it, and your house will fall to ruin;
refuse it, and your story ends.

Bee 2: Individual

A honeybee, dusted with pollen,
pushing her head deeply
into a white flower,

is the size of the moment
in which I stand and watch her.
She makes a minute seem long.

And this minute, in turn,
fills her with my foolish ideas,
until she is the size of my eye,

of my head, of the whole gingko bush
inside which she moves from blossom to blossom.

And then she is the size of what I will learn
are the roughly six weeks of her life.
As I watch, I don't know this,

or that her work outside the hive likely means
that her life is nearing its end, but I know

that this is the only moment that holds us both.
So I stay and watch her rise
from flower to flower,
the tiny petals bending under her tiny weight.

Burning Bush

Will I ever again look into fire
with the old fascination,

watch the flames leap up
the rapid air,

now that I have heard the flames speak
with their many tongues?

Or ever strike the briefest match
without that voice in my mouth—

how it ate the air around us. No,
I am married to it,

it consumes me daily.
I can't have crowded to the hearth

once, waiting to be warmed:
I'll never be cold again.

First Fruit

This fruit hides among the leaves;
it catches the eye, or the eye catches it,
the hand goes up to pluck it
and then it is in the hand,
round and perhaps a little underripe;

the eye that sees it is a golden berry
and this golden berry comes
from God and is given to God;
it is not my eye, but His;

my eye looking at you,
your eye looking at me,
must then be the eye of God
seeing us both simultaneous

Let it linger on the lip, on the tongue,
let it enter the body like a tiny pulse of light
entering the eye, like a squeeze
of the hand, like the joke

that forms in your mind and like
the sounds you use to shape it, like
the spark that it strikes in my mind, like
the laugh I let escape into the room and like

the memory of it, hanging like a berry
in some darkness among the leaves.

It Is Not in the Heavens, Neither Is It Beyond the Sea

But under my daughter's eyelid—
thinnest skin on the body.

Her eye, covered in sleep,
pivots in its bed of muscle.

My eye pivots also, to follow it.
The thinnest sign of her selfhood,

of the membrane that separates us.
She fell asleep easily beside me,

as if I were part of her, like an arm.
Her eye moves again, from right to left,

and right to left, this covers me:
I'll never see what she just saw.

Abraham and Isaac: I

I have lived in tents and know how faint a trace
we leave behind us on the earth;
how, when the body fails, the soul folds
its light clothes and steals away.

But now a child sleeps in my tent;
I would raise a tower of stone to shield his head,
and yet the thought that any common stone
must outlast him provokes such rage in me

I wake all night, alarmed and furious,
seeing nothing in the dark but dark.

Abraham and Isaac: II

I have lived in tents and often, at midday,
have I parted the tent-clothes and gone inside
with the light of day so blinding my eyes
that my wife spoke to me out of darkness,
saying, Take this dish, and eat.

I have walked among the flocks on starless nights
with the blackness so filling my eyes
I put forth my hand,
as if night were a tent,
as if some shape might glimmer in my sight
before the cloths of night fell across it.

Eyes full of light or dark,
night or day, I cannot tell.
I grope forward to lift the cloth
of this moment, and the next.

Plague of Darkness

I knew you were beside me
and yet I could not see you.
I put out my hand

and the hand seemed to disappear,
gone into the dark.
Any kind of light was a distant rumor:

a candle seemed like a long-ago miracle;
fire, like something in a dream.
I remembered the way the sky used to pale,

trembling, at the sun's approach,
and that I did not tremble then,
but waited, careless, for the lightening day.

Crossing

Familiar faces nearby are not a comfort.
Not the warm damp hand of a child,
nor the dry big one of a husband.

Not when the waters draw away from your feet.
Not when the waters rise up in a wall,
showing that there is no choice to be made.

Then it might be better among strangers,
with no one looking to you to be steady,
no one who can measure by your face

how far away the old life is.
I wanted so much to be alone. I knew
I would never be alone again.

If you've heard the walls were mirrors,
thronging with generations, this is true.
I saw a woman who looked like me,

leading a girl by the hand. I saw
the man they both belonged to.
And I understood: they were us, and not:

we were only people shuffling in the mud,
taking the path that opened up for us,
the path that always sinks beneath the waters.

Talion

What is the price of my eye?
The same as the price of his hand.

And what is the price of his hand?
The same as the price of her ear.

And what is the price of her ear?
Half a moon on a cloudy night.

A mourning dove in a forsythia bush.
Another hand folded around the first one.

Alive into Sheol

you shall know that these men have spurned the LORD
Numbers 16:30

Our dead knew us and they saw
that we had not forgotten the living.
They turned away, ashamed, hollow where we thought of

Children waiting to be settled into bed,
the softness of bedclothes, the room's dim light,
the prayers to be said together.

The prayer that rose to our lips
then was only *If we cannot go back,*
let us forget, let there be forgetting for all.

The Fear of the Dark

The fear of the dark is the flame
at the end of a match: one scratch,
and it flares.
Then a voice calls in the night.
And you go to it.

Wherever earth is in shadow,
these fears burn like fires.
This one is yours.
You tend it. Feed it a stick.
The flame crouches
to eat the wood.

Serving the fire,
you don't fear the dark.
You kneel to it,
hearing its voice
grow softer and slower, until
it says one more thing
you can't hear. And sleeps.

Chocolate

Here in a house I didn't build
I read the books I didn't write
I even eat food I didn't cook

A child grew from my body.
Released in the world, she grows on

Slaves picked cacao beans, and I—
I ate chocolate.

Manna

man may live on anything the LORD decrees

Deuteronomy 8:3

Has the time come to ask
what is suffering worth—
has it a price?

Or by what calculation we may come
to say, "It was all worth it,"
or even, "I'd do it again"?

What we are given to eat
when there is nothing to eat—
it is only a kind of dust,

Which we live on, because we must.

Turning Forty

This, they said, is a fearsome land:
No. It runs with milk and honey.
Here we can let bread rise.

Time is here. Can you taste it?
In this bread
the morning it took the dough to rise,

in these cooked apples
honey, yes, and cinnamon,
but also the hour standing at the sink,

the counter, the stove.
When we eat, we eat Time.
In this bunch of grapes,

long hours of sunlight,
long hours of night.

Alien Fire

Don't think you can select one match
from a box of matches
or lift with a matchstick
one portion of flame.

Or stretch out your hands before it,
hoping to warm them.

No bowl or brazier holds it:
your own leaking heart
the only vessel allowed.

And it is not permitted
to take one portion only.
When what the fire wants
is the whole of your hand.

Envy

It twins itself
with a matching
volume of shame,

as inside a new shoe
a proud foot blooms in blisters.

There, in Decembers of the mind,
walking, as it seems, on wounds,

and seeing—perching in one of
its empty trees—a cardinal,

I have envied it the round black eye
that spills a shield of shadow on its throat;
been jealous even of the red

that all about its breast and shoulder
rewards, rewards the bird.

Ashes

They are to carry the ashes from the altar...
                                    Numbers 4:13

Will you take the ashes from the altar though
this task consumes the minutes as the fire
consumed the offering,

though your life goes up in a blaze,
will you carry them far enough to see

the minutes on fire around you,
the hours and days aflame?

Though this task will eat a piece of every day
the ashes must be taken from the altar.
The offering is transformed—

its sacred fragrance released—its task is over,
but you will take the ashes from the altar,
your own hidden fragrance
clasped inside each cell of your body.

Jethro

When I look at a girl of thirteen,
I look at her face,
then I look at her arm growing out of her sleeve.

Supple stalk of a plant,
sleek body of a snake.

The bone of it. The muscle, tissue,
blood vessels, fat and skin, light pelt of hair.

The line starts at the eye,
then appears at the corner of the mouth.

The evil net:
We are caught in life.

And we agreed to this:
Write on us the history of our days.

Journey/Sojourn

The way a day of travel may also be
a day of stillness quiet and spent at home
moving between desk and kitchen.
Coffee cups accumulate on the white shelf

and silence accumulates in the house.
The children are at school. The writer
leans to her work. As the words pile up
and tumble slowly down the computer screen,

all the unselected words creep away into the stillness
and the work keeps on unfolding in the mind.
A trip, a journey by rail:
looking out the window at blowing wheatfields,

the telephone wires duck and rise, night comes on
and that face appears in the dark glass:
how young it was then: the line of a cheek,
two eyes full of night.

And now age is growing in her face.
Youth has gone out into the dark.
A day spent at home may indeed be full of movement,
and for a day of stillness, one may have to get in the car and go.

Emor

these are My fixed times

Leviticus 23:2

Mockingbird in rose of Sharon tree
does not want to teach me
about the shape of this moment

Or this one, in which the bird has flown,
wind moves the leaves,
leaf stirs against the earth

Mockingbird in rose of Sharon tree,
I will make you teach me
to proclaim a holy day,

mark every bee
in the bell of every flower.

3.

A Pair of Shears

*Those who died in the desert do not disappear
before the living; they lead them for a time...*

André Neher

Eve in the Garden

Six years you may sow your field
and six years you may prune your vineyard
Leviticus 25:3

When we came in August, there were roses—
budding, half opened, in bloom—
and some we had missed in their glory.
Their histories lost to us. The future is ours,
and so I took up orange-handled shears,
and all morning I severed and severed.

Whatever knotted shape the canes took
I cut away, with the small red buds
that would have been new growth.
Now, above each bush, a sphere of air.
May I be spared to cut again,
sever one future, shape another.

Spiderweb Elegy

No longer remembering why
I gathered the spiderweb
in my hand,

I can't forget the electricity
it wove between my fingers.

Those two, skin and silk,
were never meant to touch,

but when they did I felt
a crackling like hunger

in open eye and ear.
That is what made me ask—

how could anyone refuse it—
that naïve question.

A Pair of Shears

*Therefore shall a man leave his father and his mother, and
shall cleave unto his wife, and they shall be one flesh.*
                                    Genesis 2:24

All their talk was in the sound
of blade brushing blade,
a whisper of paper.
It was always exact between them.

They swung apart and met again,
pinned together at the center.
Every time they traveled back,
two edges met in the same kiss.

When that one fell, quick as a snip,
this one was left still bright and sharp,
longing to set itself against another
in the cleanest relation.

Bee 3

To look at a dead creature, however small,
A kind of prayer. You can look and look,
No one will stop you.

The way there is no end to prayers.
The way they travel out.
Going silent for a while,

Then taken up again.
A honeybee, dusted with pollen.
The stillness of its legs.

On the Past

My attention, friend, is a very small power,
sometimes tenacious, sometimes the dying gleam
of a flashlight starving on old batteries.
Yet I presume to fix it upon you

as if it were a flicker of the attention of God,
and I try with all my feeble might to strengthen it.
As yesterday, reading "The Arrow of Time,"
I read the first passage about time running backwards,

then again. "A third time will help," I thought, and it did.
Today the idea has taken root in my mind:

                              A glass of water
                    stands on a table.
        One possible future
                         is that the glass will spill.

And when it does,   that future   has a past
            in which the glass   stands upright   and full.

If I can look   at the glass   and believe   the spill exists,

then I can look   at the spill   and believe in the
                                              unspilled glass

        as utterly as if it stood before me.

As if   it had never   spilled at all.

As I continue   to   believe   in you,

                                        though the glass has fallen
        and rolled on its side,

the water poured from the table.

On Being in Other People's Dreams

As my dreaming body summons you into my dreams
so too your dreaming bodies summon mine,

and I obey—stand before you, sit, lie down,
on a bed, in a shroud, among the reeds in the river.

The things you have me say—things I would never
say if I were in my body. I say *I love you.* My hands are kites.

I cross the street to kiss the dreamer.
Dream self, stay home tonight! Don't wander

the rooms of my friends, gardens of my enemies,
of those who idly consider me from afar,

then find me looming up out of their sleep.
But even as I ask her she is elsewhere,

though the sun is high. The other side of the globe,
or someone's afternoon nap.

And one day, I die. For a while she goes on
greeting those who had thought me dead.

Some wake with tears in their eyes,
some confused, some forget the dream.

And one night she makes a last appearance—
perhaps in the dream of someone not yet born.

Perhaps in yours. She looks in at your window,
or looks at you out of mine as you walk by.

Ambulance

I have been too frightened lately,
thinking of accidents, of sudden losses,
how swiftly everything being all right

changes to something wrong;
no beautiful hour of dusk
passes without some thought of it:

even as I call my child from the street
some other family is bent in grief,
someone lifts the phone to break bad news.

But when I saw the small window
full of hospital brightness
moving quietly through the darkening day,

and inside a woman calmly on her back,
turning to one side a patient face,
eyes fastened on someone I couldn't see,

who must have been sitting at her side
and holding her invisible hand
the way she held her invisible pain,

for a moment I was comforted by it and by the thought
of the invisible driver's foot,

pressing the gas, accelerating past us.

Inquiry

C.M.H.

Let no one be found among you...who inquires of the dead
                    Deuteronomy 18:11

The years have given you back a kind of voice,
you who have been silent for so long.
You speak to me now out of earth, wind, water—
those things which do not change except in form.

The tree says, I continued to grow.
The earth says, I took more secrets to my heart.
And the water, the tireless water,
has never stopped talking yet—

> *...So much time has passed since you saw me*
> *beating the shore, and yet you are the same*
> *person who wept and lamented; you grew a skin*
> *over the wound and started to forget...*

Forgotten?—no. O voice, though I am not
the person I was when we were friends, and young,

you speak to me out of the world that is,
and I must inquire: of water, and of love,
and grief, eternity, and all the bonds

that make your world and mine, at times, seem one.

Concerning Your Death

Coming unexpectedly upon your death,
which I do once or twice a year,
is like opening a wooden door
on iron hinges
into a garden—

a private garden,
well tended;

that it was recently watered
may be seen by drops on the leaves—

or perhaps it rains here...

                    In the event,
I linger only a short time,
for the voices are coming nearer;

time to marvel at the great blooming
heads, the narrow
throats of stems—

and since I cannot
bear for long its green newness

I leave in a hurry, close the wooden door,

and never meet another visitor coming in.

Mount Nebo

I have let you see it with your own eyes, but you shall not cross there

Deuteronomy 34:4

One who dies comes to the top of a mountain
and looks over a beautiful land
she will not enter.

She knows it is not free of grief.
That shadow under the cloud is rain
that will wake the rot in the almond grove,

punish every leaf. It is right
that she should see it,
and the birds, moving their hollow bones

so quickly under the trees.

Ha'azinu

guarded him as the pupil of His eye
Deuteronomy 32:10

Had we known we were safe,
had known we were safe all along...

...as when one comes to the end of a journey
forgetting all the dangers on the way...

...greeting with almost equal delight
the growing and the breaking of the city...

Had we known that the darkness enclosing us
was the same round darkness in the center of an eye...

Had we known, we would have—
but then again, no. And yet,

it is possible to say of each life:
yes, I had one, just like you.

AUTHOR'S NOTE

"Spiderweb Elegy" is for Rachel.

"A Pair of Shears" is for E. & F.

Lines from the Hebrew Bible are from the Jewish Publication Society translation (1962) as it appears in *The Torah: A Modern Commentary*, edited by W. Gunther Plaut (Union of American Hebrew Congregations, 1981), with the exception of the epigraphs to "Ashes" (my own alteration) and "A Pair of Shears" (King James Version).

Particular gratitude to the first editors of these poems: Brendan Corcoran, Emily Pérez, Maria Melendez and Juan Morales, Alana Newhouse, Robert Pinsky and Rebekah Stout, Martín Espada for selecting the two "Abraham and Isaac" poems for *Ploughshares*, and Henri Cole for his editing of "Storm."

A Literature Fellowship in Poetry from the National Endowment for the Arts and a Rona Jaffe Writer's Award provided much-appreciated support as I began work on this book. Thanks to the Bread Loaf Writers' Conference for the Stanley P. Young Fellowship and the opportunity to be a part of the Bread Loaf community, and to the Koret Foundation for the encouragement of being a finalist for the Young Writer on Jewish Themes Award. I am also grateful to my colleagues and students at the Napa Valley Writers' Conference, the University of Southern California, and Viewpoint School for their fellowship, support and interest, particularly Amanda Clarke, Iris Dunkle, and Brighde Mullins.

I received much-appreciated readings at a critical moment from the members of my writers' group, including Laura Brennan, Danelle Davenport, Eileen Gibson Funke, Kellen Hertz, Robinne Lee, Colette Sartor, and Lisanne Sartor.

Enduring gratitude to Ellen Barber, Eavan Boland, and Lan Samantha Chang, and to my family.

About the Poet

Nan Cohen is the author of *Rope Bridge* (Cherry Grove Collections, 2005). A past Wallace Stegner Fellow and Jones Lecturer at Stanford University, she has received a Rona Jaffe Writer's Award and a Literature Fellowship from the National Endowment for the Arts.

CPSIA information can be obtained
at www.ICGtesting.com
Printed in the USA
FFOW02n1932180817
38886FF